Batik for beginners

Batik
for beginners

Norma Jameson

Studio Vista London
Watson-Guptill Publications New York

Acknowledgements
I would like to thank Eleanor Scarfe, Art Students of Coloma College of Education, and the Victoria and Albert Museum, London, for making available examples of work to be reproduced in this book; and Kenneth Jameson for his help in the preparation of the manuscript

General editors Brenda Herbert and Janey O'Riordan
© Norma Jameson 1970
Reprinted 1972
Published in Great Britain by Studio Vista Publishers
Blue Star House, Highgate Hill, London, N19
and in America by Watson-Guptill Publications
165 West 46th Street, New York 10036
Watson-Guptill ISBN 0–8230–6525–1
Library of Congress Catalog Card Number 74–119472
Set in 9 on 9½pt Univers
Printed Offset Litho and bound in Great Britain by
Cox & Wyman Ltd, London, Fakenham and Reading

ISBN 0 289 79723 3

Contents

Introduction

Making coloured patterns on cloth, by the method known as Batik, is an Indonesian art. It is a process by which areas of cloth are covered with hot, melted wax, or with a starch paste, to protect them from the coloured dyes.

Traditionally the patterns are stylized translations of naturalistic forms, delicate and complex in design. Their style originates from the decorations found in the floral patterns of the robes worn by early Javanese kings. They consist of finely drawn flowers, birds and animals. The human figure occasionally appears in pattern form, very similar in design to the well-known Javanese shadow puppets.

In Java batik designs are produced on very fine cotton material and this cloth is usually made up into some article of clothing— skirt pieces or sarongs. Fig. 1 shows a detail of a typical example of intricate pattern design based on leaf and flower forms.

Fig 1

Fig 2 Javanese batik, late nineteenth century. Victoria and Albert Museum, London. Crown Copyright

Fig 3

The Javanese apply the hot wax to the cloth by using a traditional implement called the 'tjanting' (fig. 14), and also by a metal stamping block known as a 'tjap'. Fig. 2 shows part of a skirt cloth waxed with a tjanting, and dyed indigo and dark and light brown on a white cotton ground. It was made in Java in the late nineteenth century.

Nowadays cloth patterned with a tjanting is very expensive, because it takes the artist many days to complete one piece of intricately patterned material.

India and Africa also produce wax-resisted cloth. The Indians use a brush-like implement to put the wax onto the cloth. The Africans decorate some of their materials with simple, powerful and direct designs, using printing blocks and stencils cut out of metal sheet. African cloths are noted for their blue colour, which is derived from indigo dye. Fig. 3 is a typical African cloth from Nigeria.

The art of batik is becoming widely known and recognized as an inventive medium. Western artists are using batik techniques to translate their own ideas not only into patterns designed for useful materials, but as an art form to produce two-dimensional decorative hangings.

It is a spontaneous, exciting and magical medium. It is a craft which is well within the capabilities of the non-specialist.

Equipment

Basic permanent equipment

The most important single item is some form of heater, i.e. a small electric hot-plate or a gas-ring. Place it on a non-inflammable surface while working. You will also need:

A double saucepan, or a saucepan with a tin can standing inside it, to heat the wax, or it is possible to buy an electrically operated, thermostatically controlled boiling jug. This has the advantage of heating the wax to melting point without having to use a tin can surrounded by boiling water.

A flat metal dish or tray to melt wax for use with experimental blocks, an old roasting pan will do
A tjanting
A table
Plastic bowls and/or buckets to hold dyes
Jars or bowls in which to mix small quantities of dyes
A plastic or glass measure for liquids
Spoons of various sizes
A clothes line, or some means of hanging the dyed material to drip and dry
A blunt knife
An electric iron
A pair of rubber gloves
Drawing pins (thumb tacks)
A staple-gun or a hammer

Consumable materials

Papers: newsprint or kitchen (wrapping) paper; cartridge (drawing) paper; sugar paper (very cheap drawing paper); newspapers
Wax: either household candles or blocks of paraffin wax
Grease crayons
Inks
Dyes
Cloth material: the best results are obtained on cotton or cotton-lawn. Crease-resistant and drip-dry cottons need special treatment, and are not recommended for first experiments
Nightlights (a small, thick candle).

The basic principle

The basic principle of batik is that grease and water will not mix. When a line or patch is drawn with wax on paper or material the surface is protected. If ink or dye is then used, it will not penetrate the wax. The wax resists the colour and therefore the surface of the paper or material is divided into dyed and un-dyed areas.

This makes the pattern (fig. 4).

Fig 4

Batik on paper

Drawing with a candle

There is a lot to be said for beginning your experiments in batik by trying out the methods on paper first. This will help you to understand the process. If you draw with wax on white paper, the parts covered with wax will repel the dye or ink, and the paper will remain white. So let us experiment.

We will begin by drawing with a candle, which is a convenient and easily-obtainable form of wax. All the equipment you will need for this experiment is a candle, a piece of cartridge (drawing) paper, a bottle of ordinary black ink and a paint brush.

One method is to draw on the paper with the unlit candle (fig. 5), pressing very firmly to make sure the grease is transferred to the paper; I usually use the blunt end. It is not necessary to remove the wick. Then cover your drawing with a wash of ink. It is better to try this exercise absolutely freely, without drawing in pencil first, just to get the feel of the medium. Scribble as hard as you can. It will be difficult to see the wax line on the paper, but this makes it all the more exciting when you cover your mystery drawing with the wash of ink. Paint the ink right to the edges of the paper, so that you can see your complete design (figs 6, 7).

It may be a good idea to divide your first piece of paper into sections and produce three or four experimental designs on the

Fig 5

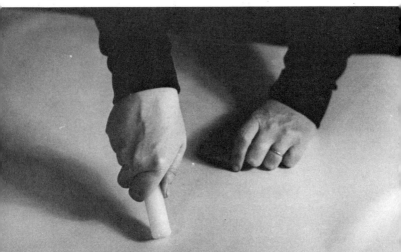

Fig 6

same sheet. Until you become accustomed to using the candle, it is helpful to be able to compare one design with another.

Fig 7

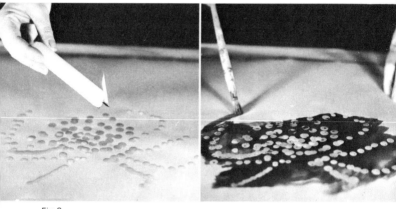

Fig 8

Another method is to light the candle and drip a design onto the paper. This makes a spotty pattern, which can be regular or irregular (fig. 8).

A third way is to hold the lighted candle very close to the paper, like a pencil, and to draw a line with the melted wax without the flame going out. When the design is complete, gently float an ink wash over the page, and your design will come alive (fig. 9).

Fig 9

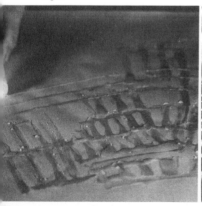
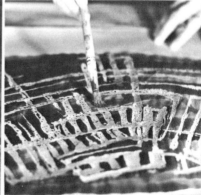

Candle rubbings

A rubbing is usually made by placing a strong, thin piece of paper–greaseproof, tracing or shelf-lining paper–on top of a textured, raised, cut, or patterned surface, and then rubbing over this with a coloured grease crayon. This makes a positive impression. I am sure you have made a rubbing of a coin with a pencil on thin paper (fig. 10). Church-brass rubbing is a favourite spare-time occupation for many people. Fig. 11 is part of a famous brass of Sir Thomas Bullen K G, 1538, in Hever Church, Kent. Fig. 102, page 96, is a batik design from this brass.

Fig 10

Fig 11

It is possible to make rubbings of textured surfaces using a candle instead of a wax crayon. Try it! Place your paper on a surface you think will make an interesting pattern. It could be frosted glass, the grid on your loudspeaker, a tree trunk, or a stone wall. Then rub your candle over it, taking care to hold the paper still, so that your design does not slip. Make sure you rub all over the surface! When it is finished, paint over the whole area with black ink. You will see that the hollows in your chosen texture or pattern become black, and the raised·pattern remains white. Fig. 12 shows a series of experimental candle rubbings.

Fig 12

When you have tried these first experiments, you will have a good knowledge of the characteristics of wax resist.

You do not have to restrict yourself to making patterns. The medium may be used in conjunction with other methods of drawing. Fig. 13 is a drawing of a bicycle made with a piece of stick and black Dylon Dye (Tintex, Rit or Aljo Batik Dye in US). The background was textured by scribbling with a candle and covering the scribble with a wash of blue dye.

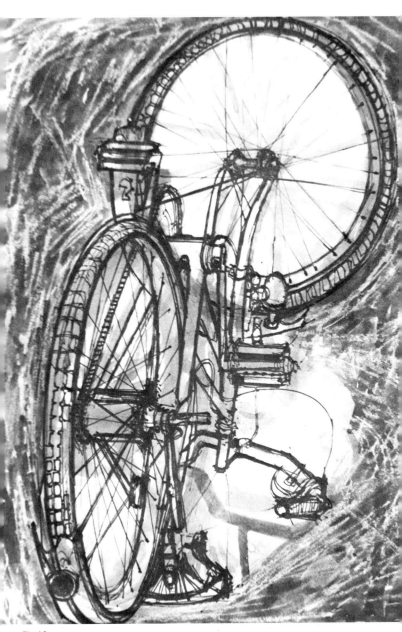

Fig 13

The tjanting

Let us go on to find out something about the traditional implements used in batik.

Fig 14

The tjanting is a tool specially designed for use with hot, melted wax. It consists of a wooden handle on the end of which is a copper reservoir with a spout. Illustrated are a number of tjantings, some bought (A, B, C); some improvized (D, E, F); and some adapted to make lines of different widths (A and B). The adaptation was accomplished by sawing off the spout and flattening the end, to stop the wax from flowing too easily.

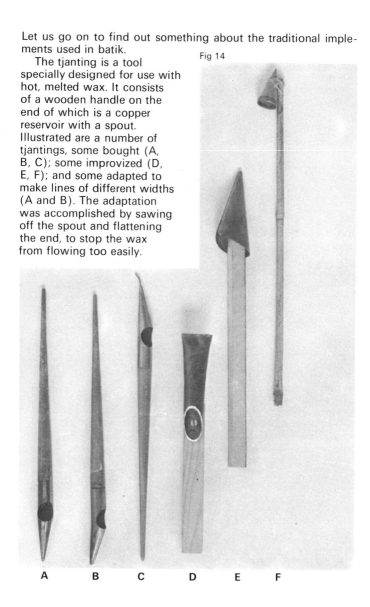

A   B   C   D   E   F

Hot wax and tjanting

EQUIPMENT
Electric hot-plate or boiling ring
Saucepan and tin can, or
double boiler
Wax: candles, or blocks of
paraffin wax
Tjanting
Cartridge (drawing) paper
Brush: decorators' $\frac{1}{2}$ in. or 1 in.

Fig 15

Place the candles or wax in a
tin can. Put the tin can into an
old saucepan. Put a minimum
of $1\frac{1}{2}$ ins of water in the
saucepan. Place it on the boiling ring and heat until the wax has
completely melted and is hot. Do not let the saucepan boil dry,
as this may cause the wax to burn. Remember that paraffin wax
is inflammable when liquid.

To begin work, submerge the reservoir of the tjanting in the
melted wax and leave for a short time until it is hot. This will help
to maintain an even flow of wax through the spout. Draw freely
to get the feel of it (fig. 16).

Your first attempts will probably be spattered with accidental
drips of wax. Ignore these until you are more experienced in using
the tjanting. When you feel confident that your drawing is relaxed
and easy, although spotty, hold a piece of paper or a tin can lid
under the spout of the tjanting, to stop the drips falling onto the
paper where they are not wanted.

A little practice will soon enable you to discover the speed at
which the wax runs out of the spout, and you will be able to
regulate your speed of drawing accordingly.

When the wax cools and ceases to flow, put the tjanting back
in the can, leave for a few seconds to make sure it is hot enough
again to restart the wax flowing, and then continue with your
design. When it is finished the wax will stand as a raised line
on the paper. Cover the paper with a wash of ink, as you did with
the candle drawing (fig. 8, page 14).

19

Fig 16

Fig 17   The completed drawing, made with tjanting and hot wax

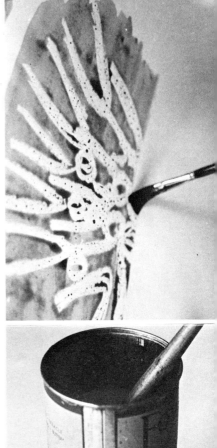

Fig 18

Hot wax and brush

The tjanting makes a fine line. When you need a thicker line, or a solid area of wax, it is much quicker to use a brush. This should be fairly floppy. There must be enough bristles to allow a good quantity of hot wax to be retained between them. This will enable you to cover a large area without having to recharge the brush too often. Size twelve is a useful size (fig. 18).

Note:
If a number of people need to use wax at the same time, it is best to heat it in small individual tin cans in a main saucepan. When the wax has melted, each small tin can be placed on top of another tin can containing a nightlight (a short, thick candle). The flame of the nightlight will keep the wax hot enough to use. The tin can with the nightlight inside must have a series of holes in the side, to allow air to circulate (fig. 19).

Fig 19

Removal of wax

To complete the process of batik it is necessary to remove the wax when the design is finished. There are two ways of doing this when working on paper. One is to scrape it off with a blunt knife (fig. 20), in which case the wax can be used again. The other way is to place the design on a pad of newspapers and cover it with a single layer. Using a hot iron, iron over the design until the newspaper is saturated with wax; then change the newspaper and repeat the process until no more wax appears. Sometimes the newspaper sticks to the design. If this happens, iron over the paper again to melt the wax, and lift the saturated newspaper as you move the iron across the surface (fig. 21).

Fig 20

Fig 21

Designing for batik

Fig 22

It is one thing to make an attractive drawing. It is another to translate it into a design for batik!

Fig. 22 is a simple drawing in black on white paper. To translate it into a wax resist, using white cartridge (drawing) paper and black ink, all the areas in the drawing which are white will need to be waxed. This means that all the shapes between the black lines, all the spaces, will be the shapes to be covered by wax. This is difficult to do, because it is much easier to see the positive black lines. For this reason it is sometimes a good idea before you begin to draw faintly in pencil the shapes which are to be waxed.

Fig 23

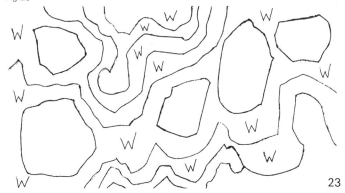

Fig 24

Fig. 23 shows these shapes marked with a 'W', to indicate where to put the wax.

In fig. 24 the solid patches were waxed with a brush and the narrow linear spaces were waxed with a tjanting. A wash of black fountain-pen ink was then floated all over the design.

It is possible to produce another design, from the first drawing, which would be a negative design. In this the tjanting would be used to wax in all the *black* lines of the drawing, instead of the spaces between them. Compare fig. 24 with fig. 25. You will see that the lines in the first design are black, the same as the drawing, whereas the lines in the second design are white.

Try translating a simple black and white drawing of your own into a positive design, and also into a negative one.

The positive and negative designs opposite were inspired by pen and ink drawings of a cross-section of a pomegranate. Brusho

Fig 25

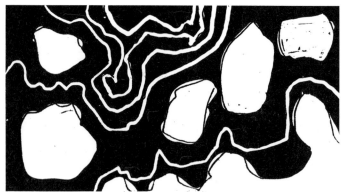

Fig 26

25

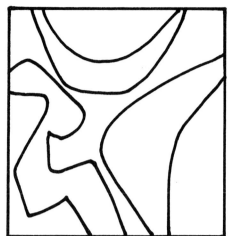

Fig 27

Watercolour Powder (use water-soluble inks in US) was used as a dye.

It sometimes happens that a drawing which looks good for translating into batik when small, looks bare and uninteresting as soon as it is enlarged. When this occurs it is necessary to be able to enrich some of the large areas with extra decoration, to make the design more exciting.

I find the most successful way of doing this is to emphasize the existing lines of the first pattern, treating these as fixed basic shapes. For instance, if you have two lines of pattern running more or less parallel, it is possible to enrich the design by drawing more lines running parallel to the two outer lines (fig. 28).

In addition to drawing parallel lines, you could fill the 'between shapes', or the shapes outside the lines, with spots, circles, or a mixture of all of these. This is the same as saying that you begin by looking at the main drawing, in order to make the first waxing; and then, virtually forgetting the drawing, let the wax design which is already on the cloth dictate the shapes of the next pattern.

Fig 28

Fig 29

Fig 30

If the pattern is basically a solid-patch pattern, the enlargement could consist of more patches growing from the central patch, with a variety of lines joining the patches together (fig. 30).

When you have experimented sufficiently with the tjanting, you will be able to enrich your patterns almost without thinking. It is a good idea to try and draw with the tjanting without taking it off the paper, except for refilling. This will encourage you to keep your design flowing.

Designs using more than one colour

More complex patterns can be made by translating drawings into designs of more than one colour. Start by mixing up three different jars of ink or dye – one light, one medium, and one dark. Successful designs are often made by using three tones of one colour – for instance pale blue, medium blue, and dark blue. These can be made from one dye. We will use this principle for the following experiment:

First mix the dye. Brusho Watercolour Powders (see page 103) are very useful for working on paper (use water-soluble inks in US). They produce clear transparent colours, and give a similar quality on paper to that of permanent dyes on material. They are *ink* powders, and not to be confused with standard powder paints. One packet of Brusho will make one pint of colour when dissolved in cold water. I usually mix one packet in a one-pound jam-jar. This gives a full-bodied colour. For paler shades either add more cold water, or use less powder. These colours will keep indefinitely in a screw-top jar. Next, starting with white paper, wax the parts which are to stay white. These will remain white throughout the procedure. Then cover all over with the light blue (fig. 31). The lightest dye is put on first, because it is easier to progress from light to dark than from dark to light. Leave it to dry.

Fig 31

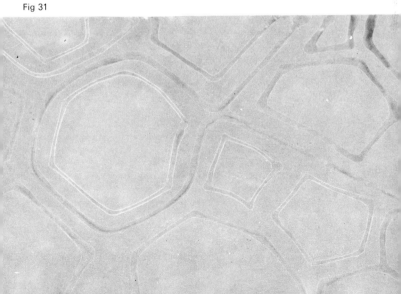

It is very important that the dye or ink dries thoroughly before any attempt is made to put on the next layer of wax. While waiting for it to dry, decide which parts of the design are going to remain pale blue. Do not forget, *the parts covered with wax will stay the colour which is under the wax*. An easy way to remember this is to say to yourself 'wax the parts to keep the colour'.

When the first colour is dry, wax the pale blue parts and paint over again with the medium blue (fig. 32). Leave to dry for the second time.

I must emphasize that it is *vital* that the dye is absolutely dry

Fig 32

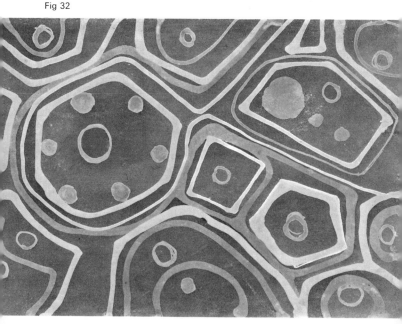

before each new layer of wax is applied. If it is not, the new layer of wax will rest on top of the wet ink, and the next lot of dye will seep under it and mix with the previous colour.

Decide which parts are to remain medium blue and cover these with wax. When the wax has set hard, paint the final dark blue dye all over (fig. 33). You can see that some of the dye rests on top of the wax in spots. These will disappear when the wax is removed.

When the design is finished and is completely dry, remove the wax – either by scraping or by ironing, as described on page 22.

Fig 33

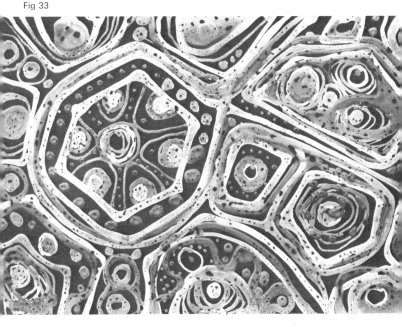

The final design (fig. 34) will be white, pale blue, medium blue and dark blue. The aim should be to achieve a satisfying balance between the four tones. Look at fig. 35; the distribution of white is very good. There is enough to make the shapes recognizable, but not too much to overpower the rest of the design.

If you would prefer to have no white at all, start your design by covering the paper with the palest colour and then continue the procedure of drying, waxing, painting until you reach a satisfactory finished design.

The design on page 33 was made from the cross-section of a loofah, in Brusho Watercolour Powder (use water-soluble inks in US) on cotton cloth. Size 3 ft × 4 ft.

Fig 34

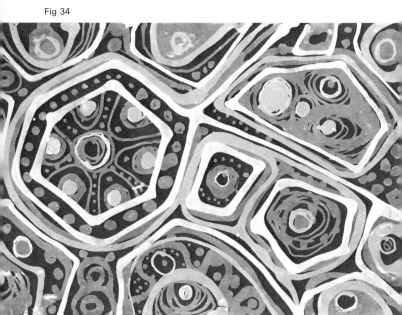

32

Fig 35

c

'Steps at a glance' for working on paper

Starting with white

1 Wax parts to stay white
2 Paint on lightest-coloured dye
3 Leave to dry
4 Wax the parts to stay the first colour
5 Paint on medium-toned dye
6 Leave to dry
7 Wax the parts to stay medium colour
8 Paint on the dark dye
9 Leave to dry
10 Remove wax by scraping or ironing

Starting with a pale colour

1 Paint pale colour all over
2 Leave to dry
3 Wax parts to remain pale
4 Paint medium colour
5 Leave to dry
6 Wax parts to remain medium colour
7 Paint with darker colour
8 Leave to dry
9 Wax parts to remain darker colour
10 Paint with darkest colour
11 Leave to dry
12 Remove wax

Batik on cloth

The most suitable materials to use for batik are pure cottons, linens and silk. They must first be washed, to remove the dressing and starch; otherwise the dressing acts as a resist and the cloth will not take dye evenly. The cloth must then be dried and ironed. It is important that it should be completely dry before you begin to wax. Old cotton sheets or pillow cases, or any odd bits and pieces of cotton, will do to practice on, but these must also be washed and ironed.

DYES FOR CLOTH

Brusho Watercolour Powder (use water-soluble inks in US)
In the previous section, in which I discussed the use of more than one colour, the ink used was Brusho Watercolour Powder. This may also be used for dying material. The colours are intermixable and give a similar quality of colour on material to that of the permanent dyes (see fig. 35). They may be painted on the cloth with a 1-inch brush, or the dye can be put into a plastic bowl and the waxed cloth immersed in it. This may entail using more than one packet of dye-powder to make the right quantity and strength of dye (about 2 pints for $1\frac{1}{2}$-yard length).

The procedure on material is exactly the same as on paper; and remember that the dye must be absolutely dry before the second and subsequent waxings can begin.

Brusho dyes (watercolour powder inks) are excellent, but when they are used on cloth they have certain limitations. They are not permanent and will wash out. For this reason they are not suitable for use on material which will be made into articles of clothing, but they are very satisfactory for wall decorations or hangings, though it must be remembered that they will fade if hung in direct sunlight. On the other hand they have considerable advantages. They are inexpensive, easy to mix, and economical for preliminary experimental colour work before using the permanent dyes. When using Brusho dyes on cloth, the wax can only be removed by ironing between newspapers, and cannot be washed out, because they are not waterproof.

Waterproof inks
Waterproof inks can be bought in 1-oz, 5-oz and 20-oz jars. They are more expensive than Brusho, but are brilliant in colour and useful for experiments. It is possible to wash material when it is dyed with these inks, but it is wiser to have it dry-cleaned. Tests should be made to make sure the colours are permanent before using them on a large scale.

Dylon Coldwater Dyes (in US, use Tintex or Rit coldwater dyes, or Aljo Batik Dye)

These dyes are permanent, easy to obtain and are very suitable for resist work, as they work when cold. If the dye is hot, it will melt the wax and the design will disappear. The procedure when using Dylon Dyes is as follows (for US readers, follow the instructions on the package of either Tintex or Rit coldwater dyes or Aljo Batik Dye):

Use 1 small packet of dye dissolved in 1 pint of warm water, and mix thoroughly. Put this into a bowl and add sufficient cold water to submerge the cloth completely. In a separate container dissolve 4 heaped tablespoons of kitchen salt and 1 tablespoon of washing soda in 1 pint of hot water and, when cool, add this to the dye bath. Put the cloth into the dye and leave it for 30 minutes, turning occasionally to make sure all the area is dyed. When dyeing is complete, dry the cloth.

If another colour is wanted, wax the areas you wish to remain the first colour and repeat the dyeing procedure. When the design is satisfactory, rinse the cloth to get rid of surplus dye. When the rinsing water is clear, cover the cloth with boiling water and detergent and leave for 5 minutes. Stir occasionally. This will release the wax. Then wash and dry the material.

Disposal of waste wax is sometimes a problem. Do not put it down the drain. It can be very useful to help the reluctant garden bonfire!

Procion Dyes, 'M' Range

Procion Dyes are clear and brilliant in colour. They mix well together. They are very permanent, simple to use, and take well on cotton, linen and silk.

The 'fixing' of the colour when dyeing cloth is usually the most complicated procedure. The 'M' Range of Procion Dyes *fix themselves*. It is only necessary to hang the dyed material in an ordinary atmosphere until it is dry. It is then fixed. This characteristic is a major advantage of the Procion 'M' Range Dyes. The standard list of these is as follows:

Brilliant Yellow M6GS	Brilliant Red M5BS
Yellow MGRS	Blue M3GS
Yellow M4RS	Brilliant Blue MRS
Brilliant Orange M2RS	Green M2BS
Scarlet MGS	Olive Green M3GS
Red MGS	Red-Brown M4RS
	Grey MGS

INGREDIENTS FOR DYEING WITH PROCION DYES

Procion Dye
Common or table salt
Washing soda (sodium carbonate)
Lissapol (use Synthropol in US): this helps to wash off surplus dye and loosen wax. See page 103 for address of supplier
Washing powder (household detergent)
This recipe will dye up to 2 yards of cotton fabric. If more dye is needed, multiply the amounts of dye, salt and soda.

Dissolve a $\frac{1}{2}$ teaspoonful to 5 teaspoonfuls of the dye-powder in $\frac{1}{2}$ pint warm water, depending on the strength of the colour you need. The dye is very strong.

In another container dissolve 5 rounded desertspoonfuls (slightly larger than a teaspoon) of cooking or table salt in 2 pints cold water. Dissolve 2 heaped desertspoonfuls of washing soda (sodium carbonate) in hot water (just enough to dissolve it) in another container. Put the dye and salt solution together in a bowl, and add the soda just before putting in the cloth. Do not forget to make sure the dye is cold before you put the cloth into it, otherwise it will melt the wax. Submerge the waxed cloth quickly and leave for 10–15 minutes. The fabric should be kept submerged, because contact with the air starts the fixing process. To obtain even dyeing, move and turn the cloth occasionally, to ensure all the surface is dyed evenly. Take the cloth out of the dye-bath and hang it up to drip dry. Do not wring the surplus dye out, as this tends to cause patchiness and uneven quality in the dyed fabric. Make sure you have a container to catch the drips (fig. 36). When the cloth is dry, the process of waxing and dyeing and drying can be repeated.

The wax will begin to disintegrate after two dips in the Procion Dye. This means that subsequent dyes will creep under the cracks and cause the dyes to merge together, making the design patchy and indistinct. To stop this, the cloth must be 'washed-off' after the second drying. To wash-off the disintegrating wax and surplus dye, rinse the cloth in cold water to remove the loose dye and then boil for two minutes in a large saucepan containing a $\frac{1}{2}$-teaspoonful of Lissapol (Synthrapol in US). Then wash in warm soapy water and dry and iron in the usual way.

If a third and fourth colour are required, re-wax the shapes already on the cloth, to protect them from the next dye, add the part of the wax pattern to keep the second colour, and continue the process of dyeing and drying.

Fig 36

Notes:

1 Once the soda has been added to the dye, there is a chemical reaction and the dye cannot be kept for any length of time. It must be thrown away after one or two hours, even though it still looks the same as it did when it was first mixed.

2 It is possible to do as many as three lots of waxing and dyeing without having to wash-off halfway through if you are careful not to crack the wax too much during the first two dyeings. Figs 87 and 105 were only washed-off at the end of the dyeing procedure. They were waxed three times.

3 The recipe for making up the dye liquid works just as well if the measures of dye-powder, salt and soda are not exactly accurate. You will soon be able to judge the quantities of salt and soda by eye.

4 If the washing-off liquid is left to go cold, the wax will float to the surface and form a solid sheet. It can then be re-used in the wax can, together with some new wax.

5 Procion Dye leaves the material soft and pliable, because the dye penetrates the fibres of the cloth.

When the final dye is on the cloth, leave it to dry for twenty-four hours and then carry out the washing-off procedure as before.

The material is now ready for use.

There are a number of other dyes which can be used in wax resist. I have not included these; either because they involve the use of acids for fixing, or because the method of dyeing the cloth is too complicated to be carried out in anything but a well set up workshop. I have chosen dyes which are easy to obtain, convenient to use and which give excellent results.

Procion dyes on cloth

Fig 37

Working on material is basically the same as working on paper. The main difference is that when you put on the wax it must penetrate right through the fibres of the material. This will ensure a clear, clean design. If the wax merely rests on top of the cotton, the dye will creep underneath the wax and the design will more or less disappear. It is easy to recognize whether or not the wax has gone through the fabric. If it has, the wax becomes dark and transparent. If it has not, it is white and opaque. The wax will only penetrate when it is hot. It rests on the top of the cloth when it is too cold. Sometimes it gets cold between taking the tjanting or brush out of the saucepan and applying it to the cloth. In order to avoid delay you *must* know the area and the pattern you are going to cover before you take the tjanting out of the pan. If the wax does not penetrate sufficiently, the other side of the material must also be waxed. This is not difficult to do if you attach the material to some kind of frame so that you can lift it up to work against the light. Some artists make a simple wooden frame before they begin, so that they can pin (thumbtack) the cotton to it and keep it taut. This also keeps the material a little way off the table and allows the wax to penetrate more easily. 1 in. × 1 in.-wood is suitable; or an old picture frame will do (fig. 60).

It is not essential to use a frame, so let us begin our first design on material by placing the piece of cotton flat on newspaper on the table, close to the pan of wax. It is essential to place the wax saucepan near the material, to facilitate quick and easy movement from the wax can to the cotton (fig. 37).

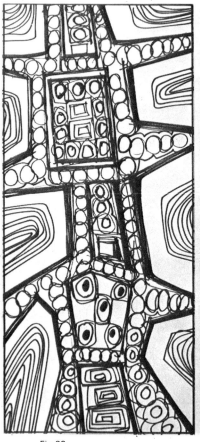

Fig 38   Fig 39

The drawing in fig. 38 is basically a decorative vertical form. It allows a variety of shapes for colour and enrichment.

It is easier, to start with, if you have some indication of the design on the material. The main shape can be drawn in with a soft pencil or charcoal before you begin. This will disappear during the dyeing processes, and thus will not show on the final design. I sometimes draw the main shapes on a piece of paper the same size as the material with a felt-tipped pen. I then place the drawing under the cotton cloth. It shows through clearly enough to see where to put the first wax. Fig. 39 shows the felt-tipped

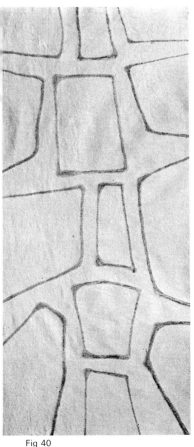

Fig 40

Fig 41

pen drawing used for the sequence which follows. It represents the basic lines taken from the design shown in fig. 38, and will serve as guide-lines.

Fig. 40 illustrates the first waxed lines, made to correspond with the lines of the drawing which can be seen through the cloth. These are the outlines of the main shapes of the design. They will now remain white throughout the dyeing process.

Fig. 41 shows the first dyeing. It is shown in black and white, but the colour was Brilliant Yellow M6GS Procion Dye. After dyeing the cloth is left to dry.

Fig 42

Fig 43

Be careful not to get the first dye too dark. It is better not to produce too much contrast with the first dyeing. Remember that you must wax the yellow areas to keep the yellow colour. The cloth is now dyed Brilliant Orange M2RS and left to dry (fig. 42).

Fig. 43 shows the cloth waxed to keep the orange colour and dyed Brilliant Red M5BS. It is dried and washed-off to remove the surplus dye and disintegrating wax and washed and ironed. Notice that the pattern is becoming richer, and that the design is gradually being built up in various parts.

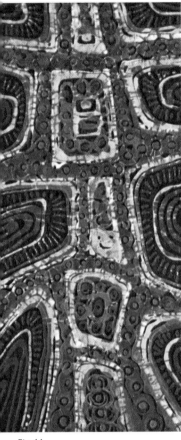

Fig 44   Fig 45

We are starting again now with the cloth washed free of wax; so it is necessary to re-wax the white, yellow and orange areas. While we are re-waxing we have a good opportunity to enrich the pattern further by waxing parts of the red areas as well. The cloth is then dyed again, in Procion Red-Brown M4RS Dye, and is left to dry for twenty-four hours at normal temperature. This simple drying fixes the colour (fig. 44). Fig. 45 shows the finished design after it has been washed-off in Lissapol (use Synthrapol in US), washed in warm water, dried and ironed.

Cracking the wax

Another difference between working on paper and working on material is that cloth is pliable and therefore the wax is liable to bend and crack as it is put into the dye. You will have noticed this. It is a characteristic of batik, and one of the recognized techniques, that you use this quality of cracking to add richness and pattern to your design. The cracks may be ordered, to a definite pattern or area, or they may be random cracks used to give a cracked texture over the whole or part of the surface.

To 'crack' the design, the whole surface of the cloth is waxed and left to go cold. In frosty weather a few minutes out in the cold air is sufficient to make the wax brittle. If the wax is brittle, the cracks will be clean and fine. If it is not cold enough outside, put the waxed cloth into cold water for a few minutes.

If the cracking is done with a piece of greaseproof paper under the cloth while waxing, instead of newspaper, it is easier to remove the waxed cloth. Sometimes newspaper sticks to the cloth and cannot be peeled off without difficulty.

The cloth is crumpled (fig. 46). It is then submerged in the dye (fig. 47). Finally it is dried and washed-off in Lissapol (Synthrapol in US), then washed and ironed (fig. 48).

Fig 46

Fig 47

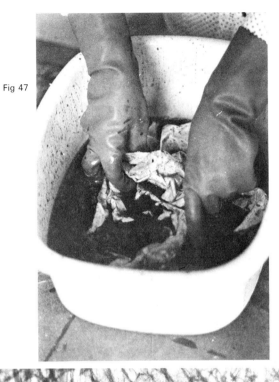

Fig 48

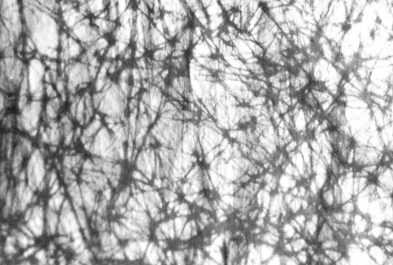

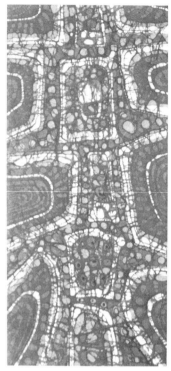

Fig 49

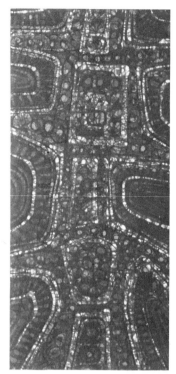

Fig 50

Fig. 49 shows the previous coloured design re-waxed and cracked irregularly all over, and dyed in Procion Brilliant Red M5BS and Blue M3GS dyes mixed together. Compare this with the last illustration (fig. 45, page 43) to see what difference the cracking has made.

Fig. 50 shows the same piece of material washed-off, re-waxed in parts, and dipped in a solution of Brentamine Fast Black K Salt (not available in US). Mix $\frac{1}{2}$–1 teaspoonful in a 1-pound jar filled with warm water. Leave to cool, put into a suitable bowl, immerse the cloth. The use of Brentamine Fast Black K Salt (see page 103 for supplier) transposes the colours into a lower key, in this case the red, yellow and orange are muted into rich, subtle browns.

It is possible after the washing-off stage to change the pattern dramatically, by waxing new shapes to keep part of the original design, and using the next dark dye to obliterate other parts of the pattern.

Controlled crack patterns can be made, when the cloth is waxed all over, by using different objects as pressure points. For instance,

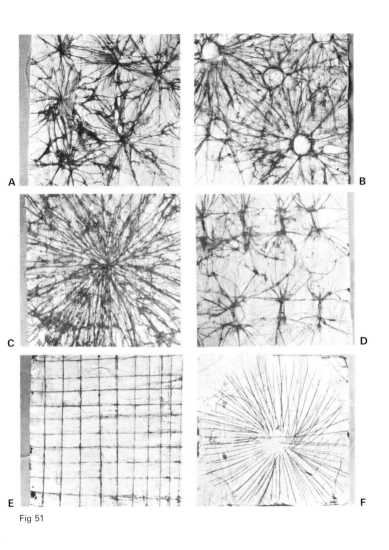

Fig 51

fig. 51A was made by pushing a pencil point at random against the cloth, screwing the cloth round the point and forcing the wax to crack. Fig. 51B was made in a similar way with the top of a bottle. Fig. 51C was squeezed round a finger. Fig. 51D was folded across the top of a ruler. Fig. 51E was folded regularly first one way and then the other. Fig. 51F was made by scratching through the layer of wax with a sharp point.

47

Fig 52

Try this experiment for yourself. See how many different kinds of crack you can make. Search out other objects and observe how they produce different crack effects.

Fig. 52 is a free translation of a design based on an eye. It is carried out in yellow, orange and brown Brusho Watercolour Powders (use water-soluble inks in US). The wax was cracked before the material was put into the dark dye. The balance of the design seemed to be improved by turning it into a vertical form. Turn the book around until the 'eye' is horizontal and see if you agree.

Painting the dye on the cloth

Some artists prefer to paint the dye onto the cloth. This gives more freedom of colour in the initial stages. If you want a yellow patch, a pink patch and a lilac patch in certain positions, it is possible to paint these patches in before waxing begins. Or you can wax parts of these patches beforehand, to retain some white, and then paint on the variety of colours. Then proceed in the same way as described on page 39, waxing and painting the cloth until the design is complete. It often makes for a more unified design when painting on the dye if the final dyeing procedure is completed by submerging the fabric in the darkest dye-bath. Liquid dye runs into the fibres of the cloth when you paint it on, making fuzzy edges. If you do not want this effect, the dye must be made into a paste form, see page 82 for the recipe. Dyes in paste and in liquid form may be used on the same piece of cloth.

Dyeing cloth from dark to light

If you would like to start by dyeing the material in the darkest dye first, cover the white material with the wax in larger areas than usual and dye the dark colour. Dry, and then boil off the wax.

Re-wax the material on the white areas, leaving some of it free of wax ready for the next dye. Dye, dry, and then boil off the wax again.

Wax the material again on parts of the remaining white areas leaving some white material free of wax to take paler dye. Dye, dry, and boil off the wax.

If more dyes are needed, repeat the processes.

This is a long-winded way of working, because the wax has to be boiled-off after every dyeing to expose more cloth for the next dye.

Mechanical aids

Fig 53

Drips of wax in wrong places can be very annoying. There are many improvizations which you can use to catch these before they land on the paper or material. An old tin-can lid, a saucepan lid turned upside down, or a piece of folded paper held underneath the tjanting as you pass it from the wax can to the design, will serve. Another way to stop unwanted drips is to cut a paper surround to cover any parts of the cloth you do not want to be waxed. Or you can just cover the part not to be waxed with a piece of paper (fig. 53).

Sometimes the accidental drips *help* the design. They can be enlarged, emphasized and made to look as though they are part of the pattern.

However, if the drip lands in a conspicuous place, and must be removed, this can be done by first scratching off the blob of wax and then dissolving the rest with paraffin.

Straight lines are sometimes difficult to do. It is possible to make accurate straight lines by using a ruler; so long as you remember to keep a gap between the ruling edge and the material, so that the wax does not touch the edge and the surface at the same time. If this happens, the wax will run under the edge of the ruler and make a 'frilly' line.

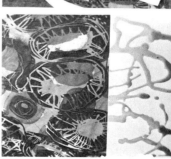

Fig 54

Stencils

If your design has elements in it which you have decided should be the same shape and size, it is easy to make a cut-out stencil shape from strong paper or cardboard (fig. 54). This can be moved over the material and used in any position you wish, waxing the shape to form the pattern.

The pattern may then be regularly spaced within the design, or dotted about irregularly on the material.

Fig. 55 shows the material dyed with a paste dye.

The Indonesians cut some of their traditional designs out of thin metal sheet. Stencils made in this way are very permanent.

Fig 55

Printing blocks

The Javanese make wax printing blocks called 'tjaps'; these are patterns made of copper strip fixed onto a block. The tjaps are dipped into a tray of hot wax and stamped onto the cotton cloth. The block thus produces a resist to the dye by leaving an imprint of wax on the surface. These tjaps allow numerous stampings to be performed on the same piece of cloth, to make a repeating pattern. This is a much quicker process than drawing an individual pattern with the tjanting on each piece of cloth. Some Javanese designs combine both techniques – part of the pattern being printed with the tjap block, and a linking meandering pattern being drawn with the tjanting between the block patterns.

The pattern objects do not have to be made from copper. They can be made from any metal items – nails, screws, nuts, bolts, spanners (wrenches), in fact any metal shapes with suitable flat faces. Fig. 56 shows a collection of such objects, which can be found in any garage odds and ends box.

When printing with these, it is necessary to heat the metal before dipping it in the hot melted wax. I usually hold the object in the hot water for a few seconds to get it thoroughly heated and dry it quickly and dip it in the wax. I then print one, or possibly two, prints per dip. Shake off surplus wax, and try to keep the object horizontal until you place it on the cloth. This makes an even print.

It is necessary to improvize some kind of wooden handle, as the metal objects get very hot when used continuously. As you see in fig. 56, it does not matter how simply these are made, so long as they are functional.

Look around for unusual metal objects, or buy yourself a small piece of sheet copper and make some interesting blocks. Metal (tin) foil, as used in the kitchen, is useful. Tear a sheet from the roll, screw it up compactly, and hammer until it is firm and solid, pushing and knocking it into shape as you hammer. Make sure that the printing surface is flat. Attach it to a piece of wood. Dip it into hot water and heat for a few seconds. Dry it and then it is ready for use as a printing block. Many different shapes can be made with tin foil. Fig. 57 shows a few examples and fig. 58 shows a print from one of the stars.

Look at the montage of prints on cotton in fig. 59 and see if you can identify which of the blocks in fig. 56 made the various patterns.

In the chapter on Procion Dyes, page 39, I mentioned the idea of working on a wooden frame, or an old picture frame. If you

Fig 56

Fig 57

Fig 58

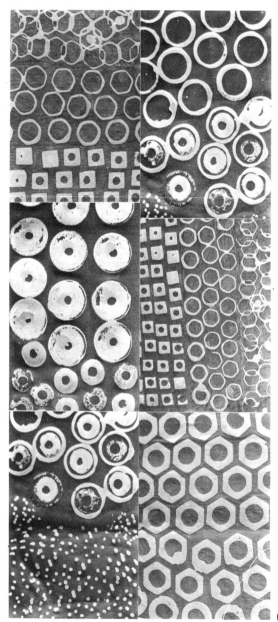

Fig 59

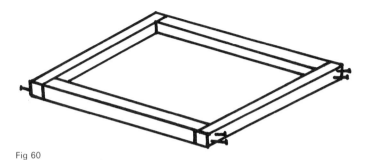

Fig 60

would like to try this, a simple wooden frame can be made from 1-in. by 1-in. wood, as in fig. 60, and the material stretched over it and pinned (thumbtacked) temporarily with drawing pins (thumbtacks). The design can then be waxed and the dye painted on, or the cloth can be taken off and dipped in a dye-bath, dried and then pinned (thumbtacked) onto the frame again for the next waxing (fig. 61).

Fig 61

Ideas for designs: starting points

What can I do? Where shall I look? Where shall I begin? These questions are often asked by the amateur. This section deals with the exciting problem of finding subjects for designs.

Let us start in the kitchen. Look in the fruit bowl and the vegetable rack. Oranges, lemons, grapefruit are all similar, both outside and inside. Cut one in half vertically and another horizontally and look carefully at the design. Choose one and ask yourself these questions: What shapes can I see? Are they regular or different from one another? How are they different? Look at the colour. Is it all the same? If not, how does it vary? And where does it vary? Try to translate it in your mind's eye into a batik. What colour would you put on first, second and third? How many colours would you use? Have you chosen to translate the whole shape, or are you going to choose just a part of it? If you have chosen a part, which part is it going to be and how are you going to decide? A useful way to help you decide which part to choose is to take a piece of paper and cut out a rectangular hole smaller than the

Fig 62   Fig 63

56

object. Place this 'viewfinder' over the surface and move it about until you find a satisfying pattern (fig. 63).

Cross-sections of apples, bananas, pomegranates, cucumbers, marrows (squash), pumpkins, peppers, carrots, beetroots, parsnips, cabbages and cauliflowers are all potential pattern providers. If you are preparing lunch, search out the patterns in the vegetables. It will provide a new interest. It will also take you longer to prepare the meal!

Do you grow giant sunflowers? These offer a clear, ready-made pattern for you to analyze, especially when the seeds are completely formed and the heads are dried. The positions of the seeds radiate from the centre in a spiral formation, and each seed has a different pattern on it. Look carefully at the lines made by the seeds, and see if you can follow their pattern from the centre of the head to the outside edge. Fig. 64 shows an analytical drawing of a dried sunflower head. Figs 65 and 66 show different designs extracted from the same subject.

Fig 64

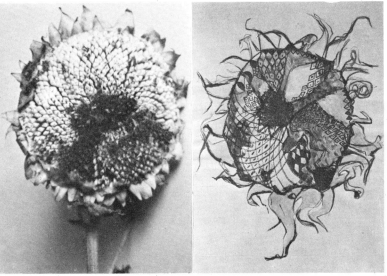

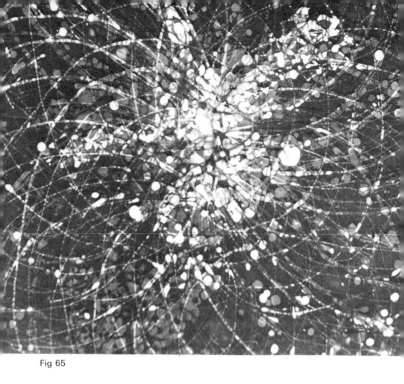

Fig 65

Fig 66

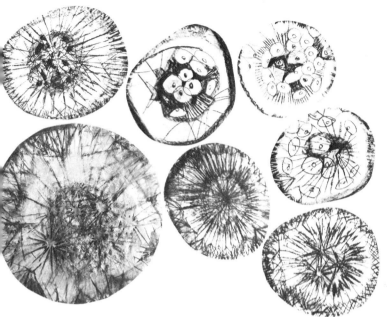

Fig 67

There are many other exciting flower forms and seed heads which will attract your attention. I find the more complex natural forms translate into the most exciting patterns.

Dandelion clocks (seed heads) have an intricate spherical construction, with tiny radial parachutes clustering together to form the outer casing and spokes joining each single seed to the centre. If you blow the seeds away, the spherical centre to which all the spokes are attached is pitted like orange peel.

You must look at each subject, and search very carefully for as much information as you can before you begin to draw and to analyze.

Surfaces are superficial. Bones are the structure. Both are vital components of design.

Find the real qualities and characteristics of your subject. Make a series of drawings before you start on the final batik. You may have missed something vital. Amalgamate the different aspects of your subject in your drawings for the final design.

Fig 68

Fig. 68 opposite is a simple batik in lilac and white on cotton. These dandelion clocks (seed heads) are a translation of the drawings in fig. 67.

Growing plant forms in relation to their surroundings make decorative designs. Take note of the shapes and textures between and beyond the plants and leaves, as well as of the plants themselves (fig. 69).

Trees have patterned, textured bark, which could suggest surprisingly colourful, and unexpectedly rich, designs. Tree trunks are not just brown. Most trunks are not brown at all. Take a closer look. Take a 'viewfinder' with a hole 8 in. × 5 in. and pin it onto a clearly marked piece of trunk. Write down all the colours you can see, draw the texture.

Your garden may be stony. Pebbles and rocks sometimes have well-defined markings. Make a collection of the most interesting ones for future reference.

Fig 69

Fig 70

A walk along the beach will reveal many fascinating specimens. Fig. 70 shows a selection of some of the objects which I found on a deserted Welsh beach. All of them have been used many times for designs and paintings.

This ram's skull made a stimulating design; the horns look like the handle-bars of a racing bicycle. When looking at this sort of subject, search out the various qualities of shape, pattern and texture. In this case the crusty texture of the horns, with the ridges and bumps, makes incidents which are valuable to translate into patterns. This wax drawing was made with a tjanting on black sugar (very cheap drawing) paper. The first waxed lines on the black paper remained black when the drawing was covered with grey waterproof ink. More lines were drawn with wax, and a lighter grey ink was used to expose these.

The background is always important, and must be considered at the same time as the drawing of the subject. It must be related to the subject throughout the procedure, and not put in as an afterthought. The background here follows the outline of the skull and sits it firmly on the ground.

Fig 71

Coloured papers are useful as variations on the procedure of starting with white paper.

There are areas in most countries which yield fossilized objects like sea urchins and corals (fig. 72); ammonites, sea lilies; and skeletons of fish (fig. 75), bird and animal forms.

Fossils are sources of inspiration for design. Visit your local museum. You never know, you may be living in an area which abounds with fossil remains which you could find yourself. Fig. 72 is a photograph of the original and fig. 73 an analytical

Fig 72

Fig 73

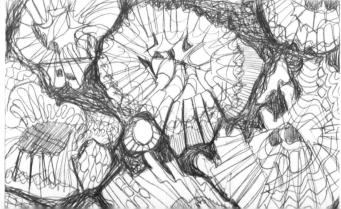

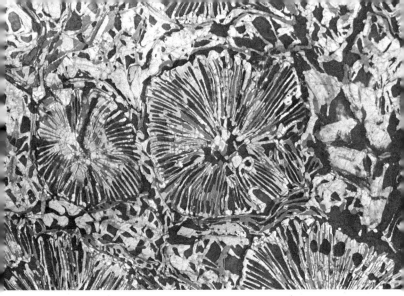

Fig 74

drawing of a piece of fossilized coral found in an ancient quarry in Durham, England. Fig. 74 is the drawing freely translated into a batik design on material.

Fossil fish forms are often found with the vertebrae broken and dispersed around the main skeleton. These are the accidental happenings which, if used inventively, make a design sparkle.

Fig 75

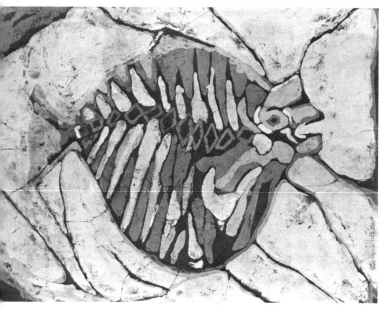

Fig 76

Fig 77

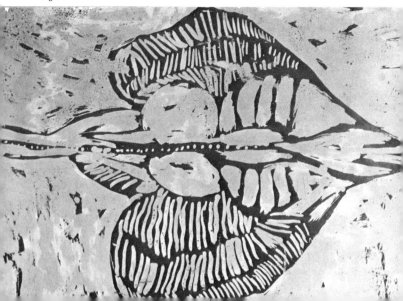

Fig. 76 is a carefully worked out, balanced interpretation of a different kind of fossilized fish form, on cotton material.

Fig. 77 is another example of a fossil fish, a powerful design in black and white, on white cartridge (drawing) paper.

Have you ever looked into clear radio valves, or clear electric light bulbs (fig. 78)?

You will be surprised at the number of subtle variations in construction you will find. Try suspending them in front of a mirror and you will get a stimulating variety of 'see-through' images, and reflections of images.

Have you looked at machinery – derelict farm machinery, modern builders' machinery, cranes, scaffolding, buildings, boats?

Have you watched the rhythm of water in stream, fountain, waterfall, wave, rain; in stillness, in frost, in ice, in reflections?

Look at the shapes and natural markings of animals, reptiles, birds, fish, insects.

Fig 78

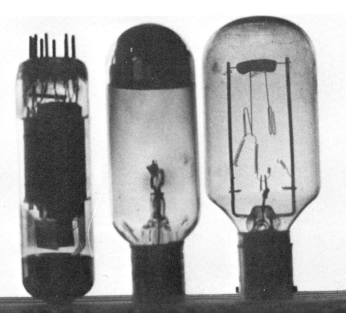

Fig 79

Fig 80

Fig 81

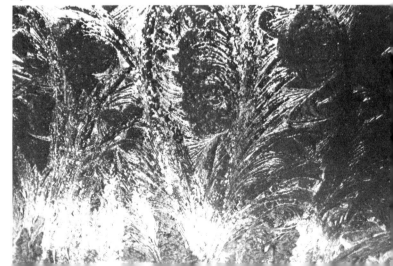

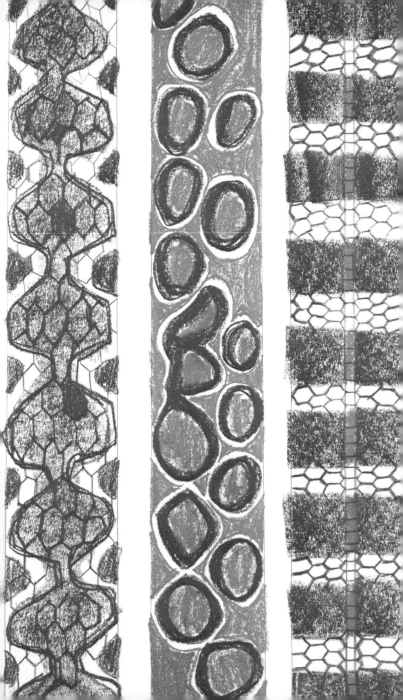

Fig 82

When you are on holiday, are you happy to take snapshots of the family, or do you find out about the local environment and record it–the fishing nets drying in the sun, the rock formations, the patterns of foliage, the textures of surfaces, the colour of the terrain, the forms of everything?

Use your camera as an aid to looking. Often there is no time to stop to make a drawing, but a searching glance through the camera's eye may result in a variety of new designs, and may act as a spur to more creative photography.

Look left, right, forwards, backwards, up, down, close-up.

Fig 83

Take a single subject or theme as a starting point. Fig. 84A, B, C, and D were all based on the theme 'fir-cone'. A magnifying glass was used to find more detail than might appear to the naked eye. Figs 84A, B, C are all the same fir-cone, looked at from below, above (notice the pattern in the background, which follows the general shape of the outside edge of the cone), from the side slightly looking down, and into the opened section of the cone.

Fig. 84D is an extension of the theme. It is based on a polished cross-section of a fossilized cone from the Natural History Museum in London. All these were dyed with Dylon (Tintex, Rit or Aljo Batik Dye in US) dyes.

Fig 84

A   B

C   D

Visual aids

Optical and other instruments can help us in the search for pattern. A magnifying glass was used for the fircones on the previous page. Photographic equipment has many accessories which can be used for the batik artist's purposes, and not necessarily for the purpose for which they were first designed. Empty slide cases, for instance, can be used to project objects like small, delicate, dead insects – gnats, lacewings – or the finely-veined wings of larger insects. You can project leaf skeletons, thin skins of garlic or onions, bits of lightweight material – nylon, net lace, nylon stockings or any other material which has a transparent or open weave – and coloured cellophane paper. These can be placed separately between the two sheets of glass in the slide cases, or a mixture of the objects can be put in together. The home-made slides can then be projected in the usual way.

If you have any film or slides which are unsuccessful as photography, either over- or under-exposed, or spoilt in other ways, it is possible to use these as experimental surfaces. You can scratch patterns with a sharp point through the surface of the negative film, or you can draw on the under-exposed pale negative with a fibre-tipped pen and project your trial designs.

Interesting patterns can be caught if photographs are taken as time exposures in the dark, especially during firework displays, when the pattern of cascading stars falls haphazardly in the black background. Sparklers held in the hand and twisted and moved around in erratic lines make excellent eccentric designs on film.

If you are an enthusiastic photographer and have enlarging equipment, it is possible to use actual natural objects in the enlarger and to project these on to sensitive photographic paper. By this method an imprint will be left, and maybe a new design will take shape. The same sort of objects can be used here as can be placed between the slide cases – nets, skins, insects, grasses, feathers, etc.

Thin cross-sections of the stems of plants can be cut, stained, and placed on glass slides and looked at through a microscope. Photographs of these sections can be taken if you have proper equipment. Photographs of microscopic insects can also be taken this way. These photo-micrographs often produce beautiful, intricate, lace-like patterns. This type of photography opens up a new world, a world which is not normally seen by the naked eye. It is magical and unexpected.

All the above images, whether projected or observed under magnified conditions, can be used for making preliminary studies, using any kind of drawing implement. The list of drawing instruments is considerable; it includes pencils, ballpoint pens, felt-tipped pens, pastels, oil pastels, chalks, charcoal and reed pens and other experimental drawing implements – such as twigs, sticks, or dead flower stalks used with black ink or dye.

You will have your favourites among these, no doubt, but it is a good thing to experiment with as many of them as possible. If you have access to a microscope, look at biological specimens on slides and try to translate them into drawings.

If you make a large detailed drawing (fig. 85), it is possible to subdivide it by isolating sections of it with a viewfinder, so producing any number of designs, a dozen for the price of one. Fig. 86 shows the same drawing with a number of viewfinders showing possible designs. The drawing was made with a felt-tipped pen.

Fig 85

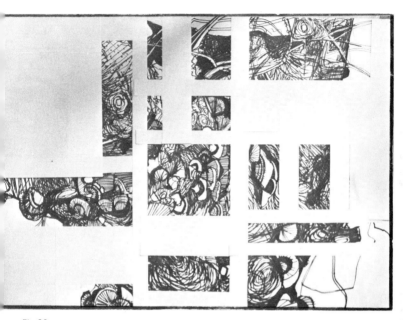

Fig 86

Fitting the design to a rectangular shape is sometimes awkward, especially when all the interesting bits happen round the outside edge and leave the centre bare, or when everything occurs in the middle and the rest is boring. If you are making a decorative hanging it is usually best if the most significant part of your design is slightly off-centre vertically and horizontally, and above or below the halfway line.

The variety of starting points is endless. In this section I have indicated a number of possibilities. You will have your own ideas and interests. Do not be afraid to try them out, however complicated and impossible they may seem.

Colour

Experimenting with colour is the only way to learn about the reaction of the dyes to each other. It may be a useful exercise to make a series of tests before you begin any serious piece of work. Keep a record of the quantities of dye-powder that produce certain strengths of colour, so that you will eventually build up a reference to all the colours you have used. If you ever need to reproduce a colour exactly, it is vital that you use the same quantities. Even a slight variation in the amount of dye-powder will produce a different tone.

Colour is personal. You may like delicate pastel shades, or rich glowing colour; warm tones – pinks, oranges, reds, browns, purples – or cool tones – blues, greens, greys – or families of colours.

Whichever your preference, find out what happens when you put blue over yellow, yellow over blue, green over red, orange over purple, red over blue, blue over green. Be daring and try out what might seem unlikely as combinations of colour. Unusual, original, subtle works may be the result of an uninhibited experimental approach to colour.

Remember that only the first colour which you wax over will remain pure.

How do you make green? This is a question which is often asked by school children. One answer is 'which two colours in your palette do you think are nearest colours to green?' It is more significant to the child if, by looking and analyzing the colours in the palette, he finds for himself the two needed to make green. Green is much more complicated than just any green. It could be pale, medium or dark; or yellow-green, blue-green, grey-green, olive green; and you could go on to emerald, apple, leaf, laurel, and the innumerable slight variations found in natural forms in summer.

All colour can be analyzed in this way.

By adding the slightest quantity of dye-powder to a basic colour you will change its character.

Try mixing up a basic pink colour and add in turn tiny amounts of all the other dyes to see how the basic pink is changed – e.g. pink and yellow, pink and orange, pink and red, pink and brown, pink and green, pink and blue, and so on.

Do not stint on the selection of the dyes you buy. The sight of the colour standing in the jar is a stimulus which will jog your visual awareness of its relation to other colours and its potential as a 'colour changer'.

Different coloured tissue papers are useful when testing one colour against another. They can be glued down very quickly

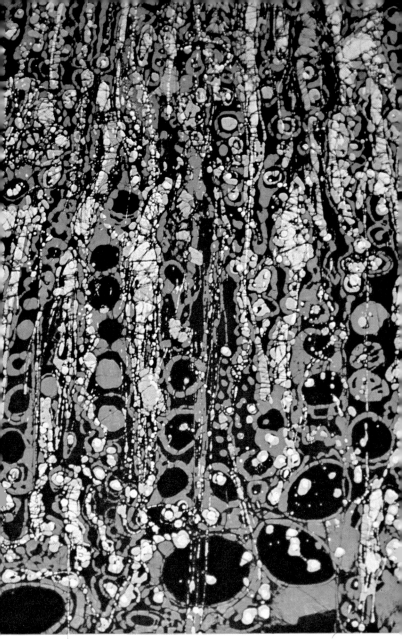

Fig 87 *Purple Pool*, a batik on cotton. This shows translation of wetness and watery atmosphere rather than the study of an actual pool

with Polycel (UK) which is a type of wallpaper paste, using one teaspoonful to a pint of water. This will give you some idea of what one colour will do to another when placed over the top of it. Designers often carry out their preliminary drawing in another medium before attempting the final batik. Transparent coloured cellophane can also be used. This needs a different adhesive to stick it down. Clear Bostik (use Elmer's or Sobo in US) is excellent, or you can stick it onto transparent Fablon (UK), which has a self-adhesive back. Coloured acetate sheet can be used in the same way. It is expensive, but is fun to play with. There are some transparent coloured plastic building kits for children which are also exciting to use from the point of view of experimenting with 'see-through' colour (fig. 88).

Colour in batik can be imaginative and unique. *You must experiment.*

Fig 88

Other resists

Wax is only one of the substances used in resist dyeing. Some Javanese and Nigerian textiles are dyed using cassava starch paste as the resist. This is freely painted onto the fabric, or applied through a stencil cut from thin metal sheet.

A substitute paste resist can be made from flour and cold water, mixed to a creamy consistency (fig. 89).

It is probable there are many new pastes and gums on the market that could also be used for resist work. Experiment with some of these to find out whether it is possible to use them.

I have found flour and water paste the easiest substitute resist to use. This is cheaper than wax, and somewhat easier to work with at home. You can spread it over a large area with a brush or, better and quicker, with a blunt smooth knife. Or you can put it into an empty plastic detergent dispenser and force it through the nozzle by squeezing (fig. 91). This will make a fairly fine line, providing the flour and water is mixed to a really smooth consistency. If the mixture is lumpy, the nozzle gets blocked very quickly and it may be necessary to make the hole in the nozzle bigger. This, of course, will make the line thicker.

The paste rests on the surface of the cloth and it is important to wait for it to dry hard before any attempt is made to dye the fabric. It is best to leave it overnight, on a flat surface. Be patient, and do not be tempted to paint the dye on before the paste is really hard.

Fig 89

Fig 90 Analysis of the structure and surface patterns and textures of rock formations. Notice the different coloured crackings

Fig 91

When the flour and water paste is dried and hard, the cloth can be screwed up and cracked in the same way as wax. This sort of resist produces very incisive lines (fig. 94).

Using the detergent bottle as a trailer is rather like putting an icing pattern on a cake. It is possible to use icing-sugar forcing bags; or metal ones as in Fig. 91.

Since the paste resist rests on the surface of the cloth and does not penetrate right through the fibres, and since it is a water-bound resist, liquid dye would soften and creep underneath the paste, and the cloth would become a solid soggy mess of blurred pattern and gooey paste.

It is essential then to use a dye which will not soften the flour-and-water-paste resist. It must also be a dye which can be painted onto the cloth, because the pattern made by the resist is on the top surface only. If the cloth were submerged in liquid dye, the back of the pattern would become coloured and the material would be dyed all over. So you will need a paint brush, a 1-in. house painter's brush, or a foam rubber sponge.

A different recipe is used to make up the dye in paste form. Using the same Procion Dye, the recipe is as follows:

INGREDIENTS

Calgon (water softening powder)
Manutex (a dye thickener; use Keltex in US), see page 103 for supplier
Cold water
Urea (helps the dye to penetrate the cloth), see page 103
Hot water
Dye-powder
Resist Salt 'L' (use Sitol Flakes in US), see page 103
Bicarbonate of Soda

1 2-pound jam jar (2 pints approx).
1 1-pound jam jar (1 pint approx).
Teaspoon
Tablespoon

MAKING THE BINDER

To make the Manutex (Keltex) binder, which thickens the dye, dissolve a desertspoon of Calgon in a 2-pound jar (approximately 2 pints) of cold water. Steadily add a level tablespoon of Manutex and stir for a few minutes until it thickens. Leave until it becomes transparent. Once mixed this binder will keep for several weeks in a screw-topped jar.

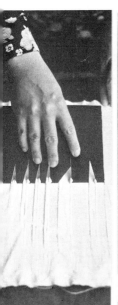

Fig 92

MAKING THE STOCK PASTE DYE

Fill a 1-pound jar (1 pint) a quarter of the way up with Urea. Add hot water to bring the level up to halfway mark and dissolve. Stir in 2 heaped tablespoons of dye-powder. This makes a strong colour. Add one teaspoonful of Resist Salt 'L' (Sitol Flakes) and fill to the top of the jar with the Manutex (Keltex) binder, prepared as above. Beat the mixture well with a spoon until it is smooth like syrup.

The mixture is ready for use when the bicarbonate of soda has been added. Remember that this limits the life of the dye. It is therefore practical and economical to add the bicarbonate of soda to small quantities of dye-paste, as it is needed. Convenient quantities are about a $\frac{1}{2}$ teaspoonful to 2 ounces of dye-paste.

It is sensible to make a number of different coloured printing-pastes, or stock dyes, so that intermixing is simple and convenient. It is more economical to add darker colours, in small quantities, to lighter colours than vice versa.

Fig. 92 shows another possible way of working with flour and water resist. If you cover the piece of material completely with the paste you can then scratch through, and scrape off some of it, while it is still wet. Stripes and checks can be produced in this way.

When the paste has dried overnight, the cloth can be dyed. The

Fig 93

dye is painted or sponged onto the cloth (fig. 93). Make sure it penetrates through any cracks in the paste which are relevant to the design.

Leave the cloth to dry for twenty-four hours. If another dye is required, repeat the pasting, drying, dyeing process. When you have sufficient colours on the design and the cloth is absolutely dry, the paste can be picked, flicked, rubbed, or scraped off.

To fix the dye, iron the material on both sides for about five minutes with a hot iron or a steam iron.

After fixing, the material should be rinsed in cold running water to remove all surplus dye. Then it should be boiled for three or four minutes in a solution of Lissapol 'D' Powder (use Synthropol in US), a $\frac{1}{2}$ teaspoonful of Lissapol 'D' (Synthropol) to a large saucepan of water. It is then ready to be washed and ironed.

Fig. 94 shows a collection of paste-resisted cloths with parts of the hard paste left on. The pattern is revealed when the resist is removed.

Fig 94

I think it is wise, at first, to use only one make of dye and so get thoroughly knowledgeable about its characteristics before experimenting with others. I like Procion Dyes. Once the recipes are known they are easy to use both in liquid and in paste form.

Printex Dyes (sold in the US under the brand name Verstex)

Another range of dyes suitable for use with paste resist is known as Printex Fabric Printing Colours (Verstex in US). These are obtainable in convenient quantities from Winsor and Newton Ltd. They consist of jars of concentrated, intermixable, pigment dyes and a binding paste. The dyes must not be used alone. They must always be used in mixture with the binder.

This range of dyes also includes a white printing paste.

It will be seen that this extends the possibilities of the medium in two important ways: it can be mixed with other colours, thus making them lighter and opaque, and, a more important point, the white dye makes it possible to overprint light colours on dark areas. If you would like to try these dyes with paste resist the method, to dye one yard of cotton material, is as follows:

First wash and thoroughly rinse the cloth.

Add 1 teaspoonful of pigment to approximately $\frac{1}{3}$ pint of binder. Both must be thoroughly stirred before they are mixed together. The pigment is very strong, so mix the colours carefully. If you require pastel shades use less pigment. The dye can be painted or sponged onto the cloth.

When the dyes are dry and the design complete, the colour is fixed by ironing the material on the back, after removing the paste resist. Iron for three or four minutes per square foot, with the iron set at the temperature suitable for the cloth. The dye will become more permanent as you go on, so if you can bear to iron for longer than four minutes per foot do so. Wash the cloth gently in detergent, rinse well, and hang to drip dry. Then iron again and it will be ready. No further processing is necessary.

Paste resist is a very good resist for children to use, because it does not involve hot stoves, molten wax, or boiling water.

The design in fig. 95 is *Apple Tree*, a four-colour design on cotton in paste resist, using Printex Dyes (Verstex in US) in pink, red, purple and brown. Size 22 ins × 30 ins.

The cloth was pinned to a wooden frame throughout the procedure. You will see that the main areas of the first paste resist were the four corners and the large areas of blossom. The paste

Fig 95

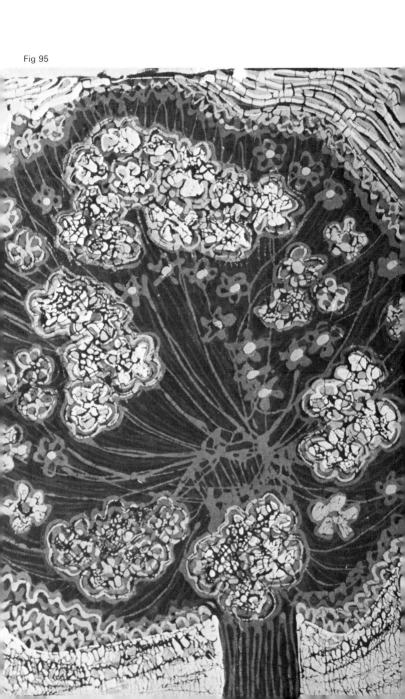

for these was applied with a plastic detergent container, as in fig. 91, and left to go hard overnight.

Half of a 1-pound jar of dye-paste was mixed for the first pink colour. This was then applied over the hard-dry flour and water paste with a large paint brush and left to dry. Resist paste was then applied to keep the pink.

To make the second colour, a little red dye-paste was added to what remained of the pink. This produced a light red. This was then painted on and left to dry. Paste was again added, this time to retain the red. Half the quantity of dye-paste was still left, so purple was added to this to make the third colour, and brown was added to the residue of dye to make the fourth and darkest colour. The dyeing and resisting was repeated as for the first and second colours.

Using up scraps of paste-resisted cloth to form highly-patterned, strange, atmospheric, magical, imaginary decorations is a good way of extending a simple experimental beginning in a new direction—a step further. Experiments are useful in themselves as records, but are more often than not discarded and thrown away. It is interesting to see if they can be used again creatively, fitting patterns together or cutting them to fit another larger shape. They can be joined by sewing, or glueing with Copydex (use Sobo in US), to form decorative pictures—kings, queens, cats, dragons, fish, palaces etc.

Extensions of the batik process: combining batik with other media

Batik is an art in its own right, but it should not be forgotten that material dyed by this method can be used in conjunction with other media. A piece of material which has on it only a batik crack pattern can be used as a base for stitching on beads to make a focal point of design. It can be used as a base for embroidery, by adding details – using a variety of threads and stitches – or as a background for using new materials, such as nylon line (fishing line), coloured acetate sheet, plastic mirror paper etc., as in fig. 96.

A batik design can be planned as a basic design or texture to combine with a screen print. When this is done, the screen print is used to obliterate some areas of the batik. This process must take place when the batik material is completed. Procion Dye in paste form can be used for screen printing.

Another possibility is to buy an already-patterned material and to use that as a base for a batik. The dyes you use must be tested on the commercially dyed cloth before you start, to make sure they are compatible.

A piece of batik material can itself be cut into shapes and these can be appliquéd onto a plain, patterned or coloured material.

Other combinations are possible. Knitted, crocheted, woven, string patterns can all be incorporated.

All these designs must be planned in advance.

Keep your standards high. It is a mistake to think that an unsuccessful design in batik can be improved by the addition of 'buttons and bows'.

Fig 96

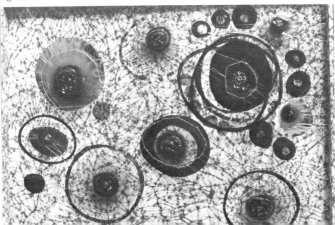

Framing

Framing the decorative materials you have made is simple. There are a number of ways of doing it. A wooden frame of the simplest kind should be made slightly smaller than the material, so as to allow for a turning of about $1\frac{1}{2}$ ins all round. 1-in. square wood is suitable for most sizes. There is no need to mitre the corners. Make the frame as in fig. 60, page 55. Then place your design face down on a flat surface. Put the wooden frame on top of it, fold the material round and pin (thumbtack) it onto the wood with drawing pins (thumbtacks). When you are sure it is in the right place, and stretched fairly tightly over the frame, tack the material permanently in position with a hammer, or you could use a staple-gun. Try to get the folds at the corners as neat as possible. If you accomplish this successfully you may find you do not want an outer frame, and in addition the design will be continuous from the front round to the sides (fig. 98A).

If you feel a more complicated frame is called for, a wooden batten (thin wooden strip) $1\frac{1}{2}$ ins $\times \frac{1}{2}$ in. may then be nailed in place around the outside edge of the previous simple frame (fig. 98B). This surround can be mitred, or not, as you wish.

If a more 'de luxe' finish is required, aluminium strip (1 in. $\times \frac{1}{8}$ in.) screwed onto the outside edge of the first simple frame makes an attractive modern surround (fig. 98C).

If you intend your design to be a wall-hanging, it will be necessary to turn in, and sew, all round the edges; unless the selvage of the material is on the two vertical sides. If it is, then you will only need to stitch the top and bottom of your design. If you turn in the top and bottom about 1 inch it will then be a simple job to insert a narrow dowel rod through top and bottom hems (fig. 98D).

Fig 97

A   B   C   D

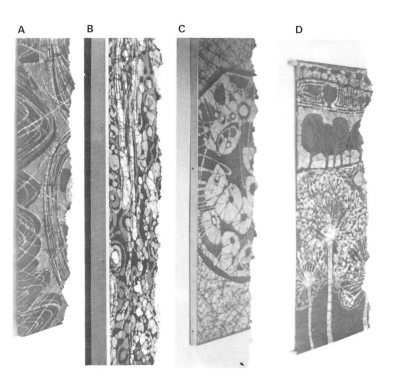

Fig 98

Lengths of material

You may wish to produce lengths of material for practical use.

As in all methods of patterning material, if permanent dyes are used the cloth can be made into curtains, sunblinds, chair-covers, cushions, bedspreads, lampshades, dresses, scarves, ties, soft toys, etc., with no fear of the dyes fading.

Some thought must be given to variation in scale when deciding what kind of pattern to put onto curtains or dress material or material specifically designed for a bedspread. Large patterns may look perfect on curtains, but may not be so suitable for dress fabrics.

Many points need to be considered when designing for a special purpose – position, colour, scale, proportion, size, line, texture, shape, associated objects. Take into account the exterior and interior aspects, for example in the case of curtains. Do not design lengths of material 'in isolation', in the hope that you will find a use for them. Start with some basic idea about future use.

If you want to make dress material, it is best to batik the complete piece of material before cutting out the pattern. This allows for possible shrinkage during the dyeing process.

If you are working with children it may be a good idea to make the session into a group activity. Every child produces a small piece of decorated material, which can then be used to form part of a combined work, by stitching the separate pieces together, or by using them as appliqué motifs. Bits and pieces cut from the ends of fabrics could be used to make patchwork quilts, or puppets.

The bow ties in fig. 99 were all made from ends cut from decorative hangings after they had been framed. You need about a 6-in. run of 36-in. material to make a bow tie.

Fig. 99 shows a selection of examples of uses which can be made of batik material.

Fig 99

A series of designs

Fig 100

On this and the following pages are a number of batik designs in the form of decorative hangings, based on a variety of subjects.

A carefully planned batik showing two vertical dark shapes against a light cracked background. The idea was derived from looking at eroded rock formations on a Cornish beach. Brusho Watercolour Powder (use Tintex or Rit in US). 4ft × 3ft.

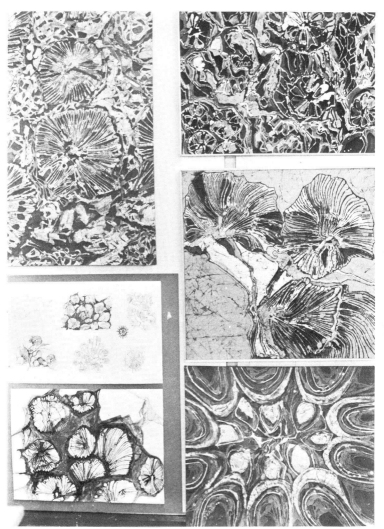

Fig 101

Fig. 101 shows a series of studies based on a single theme, coral forms, made by a student in her third year at a college of education in England. The three designs on the right were carried out by painting the dye on the cloth. The centre right was dipped in the last dark dye to make the slight cracking in the background. Average sizes 3 ft square. Procion Dye.

Fig 102

Fig. 102 is a transcription from a rubbing made from the brass over the tomb of Sir Thomas Bullen K G, 1538, in Hever Church, Kent. The effect is produced by one dyeing; brown on white, with extensive cracking. Size 4 ft × 3 ft.

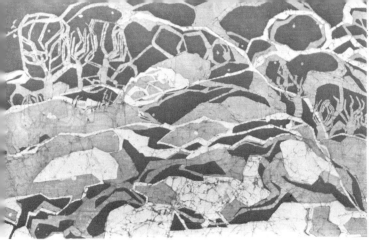

Fig 103

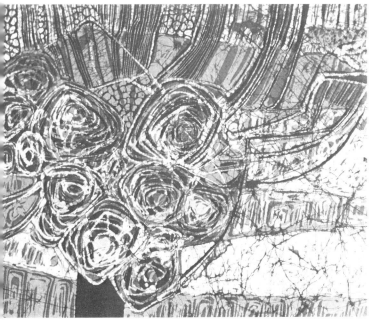

Fig 104

Figs 103 and 104 use landscape motifs as the basis of their designs. Fig. 103 was a broad view of rolling countryside, whereas fig. 104 takes a close look at one pollarded laburnum tree. Both designs were carried out in various tones of green.

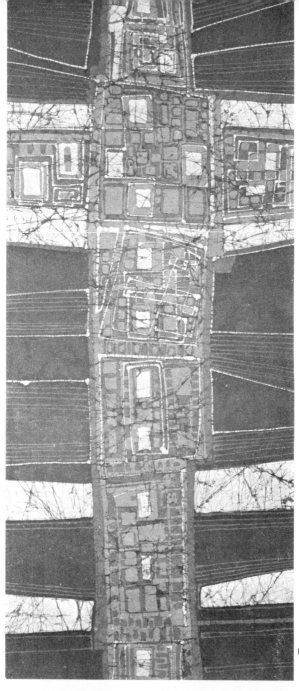

Fig 105

Fig 106

The opposite panel was designed as the centre part of a triptych. The cruciform design was constructed around a vertical motif and dyed in lilac, orange, red and red-brown Procion Dye. The rectangular forms in the background were left fairly empty, to create a quiet effect against the elaborately-patterned cross. Size 6 ft × 3 ft.

Fig. 106 employs a more literal approach to the subject matter. Lilac, pink, red and purple Procion Dyes were used. The vase and bouquet were drawn very freely with a tjanting. There is no reason why you should not produce patterns which are representational, if that is what you prefer.

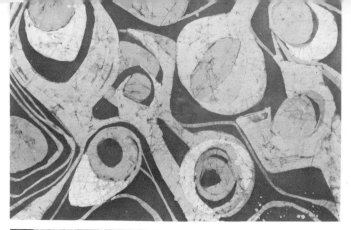

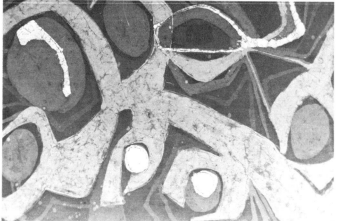

Fig 107

Two very similar versions of a small part of one cross-section of a pomegranate, emphasizing solidity of shapes. The main areas of wax were put on with a brush. The artist became fascinated by the variation of colour in the pomegranate as its surface began to dry and wither.

A batik specifically designed to hang over a glass-panelled door: fig. 108 shows a section of the design, illustrating the use of a stencil with rectangles of various sizes. This makes the central vertical column in the first pale colour. Spots and parallel lines are used to decorate the outside edges, and finally irregular cracking all over the design integrates and unifies the pattern. Brusho Watercolour Powder was used for this temporary hanging. You will remember that these dyes are not permanent. You can see where the colour is beginning to fade in the top right hand corner.

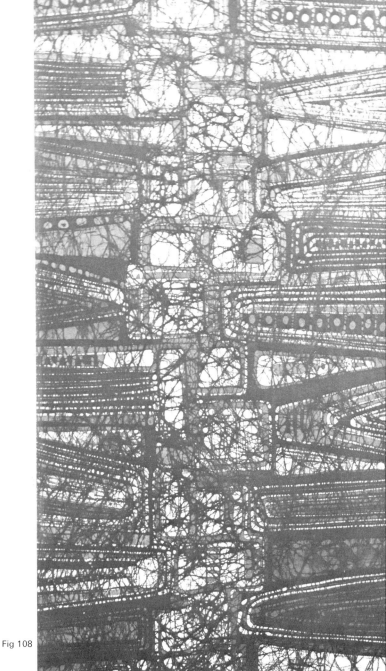

Fig 108

Conclusion

In the beginning of this book we experimented by drawing patterns with a candle on paper. Artists like John Piper use this technique as a means of obtaining interesting textures in their drawings. Candle rubbings and scribblings can be used to suggest different surface qualities of buildings, landscape, etc.

From drawing with a candle to making complex designs of more than one colour using the traditional implements of batik is a complicated progression, but this is only a beginning. With more experience and an experimental outlook, you can go further into the problems of designing, and finding and searching out other exciting subjects.

Train yourself to be aware of design in everyday life, especially in the natural world. Be interested in everything. Be curious. Investigate the world of pattern.

You do not need to be an expert draughtsman to produce good designs. Explore the possibility of designing in less usual materials, such as pastels, tissue paper or coloured cellophane. Do not limit your horizons by imagining that you must only translate *drawings* into batik. Use photographs, illustrations, diagrams.

Do not always be tempted by pretty things. It could be that a more unique pattern will develop from an unprepossessing object.

Try combining all the wax techniques together, tjanting drawing, nut and nail prints, stencils and cracking, to make a single unified design.

In the same way combine all the qualities of paste resists—trailing, combing, scratching, scraping, and cracking.

Batik is a traditional craft; its technique can be extended, by new thought and different emphasis, from functional decorative fabrics to unusually-designed wall-hangings.

As you experiment and record your ideas, your confidence will grow. Start in a simple way. Be patient, and gradually build up a body of knowledge and experience. This is the way to improve your technique, to develop your sense of design and finally to achieve mastery over the medium.

List of suppliers

List of suppliers (England)

Brusho Watercolour Powders: J. B. Duckett & Co., Sheffield 8

Candles and nightlights: grocery shops
Cotton material: Dryad Handicraft Ltd, Northgates, Leicester. Emil Alder, 46 Mortimer Street, London W1. Bradley Textiles Co., 15 Stott Street, Nelson, Lancashire

Dyes and other chemicals (including Lissapol, Brentamine Fast Black K Salt, Manutex, Urea, Resist Salt L, Lissapol D Powder): Mayborn Products Ltd, Dylon International Ltd, Oxford Works, Worsley Bridge Road, London SE26

Printex, or Tinolite Pigment Colour: Winsor & Newton Education Division, Wealdstone, Harrow, Middlesex

Tjantings: Dryad Handicraft Ltd, Northgates, Leicester

Wax (blocks of batik wax): Dryad Handicraft Ltd, Northgates, Leicester

List of suppliers (USA)

Candles: supermarkets, department stores, specialty shops, etc.
Cotton material: fabric shops or fabric department of department stores

Dyes and other chemicals: Craftools Inc., 1 Industrial Avenue, Woodridge, New Jersey (mail order). Fezandie & Sperrle Inc., 103 Lafayette Street, New York, N.Y. (mail order). Arthur Brown & Bro. Inc., 2 W. 46th Street, New York, N.Y. (no mail orders under $10.00)
Tintex and Rit Dyes: any supermarket or hardware store

Tools and wax: most art supply stores, or order from Craftools Inc., or Arthur Brown and Bro. Inc. (addresses above)

For further reading

Batik by Nik Krevitsky; Reinhold, New York 1965
Batik. A survey of batik design by A. Steinmann; Leigh on Sea 1958, published by author
Batiks by John Irwin and Veronica Murphy; Victoria and Albert Museum, London 1969. Obtainable through HMSO
A bibliography of dyeing and textile printing by L. G. Lawrie; Chapman and Hall, London 1949
Dyes and dyeing by Pat Gilmour; Society for education through art, 29 Great James Street, London WC1 1966
Fabric printing by hand by Stephen Russ; Studio Vista, London 1964; Watson-Guptill, New York 1964
Introducing batik by Evelyn Samuel; Batsford, London; Watson-Guptill, New York 1968
Textile printing and dyeing by Nora Proud; Batsford, London; Reinhold, New York 1965
The following leaflets are obtainable free from Mayborn Products Ltd, Dylon Works, London SE26: *Textile printing with Procion Dyes, Tye and dye, This wonderful world of colour (Dylon Dyes)*

Index